STUDY PLANNER

D -

MOOD ☺ ☺ ☺ ☹ ☹	DATE.		MON	TUE	WED	THU	FRI	SAT	SUN
TODAY'S PRIORITY									
○									
○									
○									

PLAN

		○
		○
		○
		○
		○
		○
		○
		○
		○
		○
		○
		○
		○
		○
		○
		○
		○
		○
		○
		○

TOTAL TIME	H	M
6		
7		
8		
9		
10		
11		
12		
1		
2		
3		
4		
5		
6		
7		
8		
9		
10		
11		
12		
1		
2		
3		
4		
5		

COMMENT

STUDY PLANNER

D -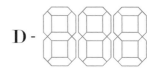

MOOD ☺ ☺ ☺ ☹ ☹	DATE.	MON	TUE	WED	THU	FRI	SAT	SUN

TODAY'S PRIORITY

- ○
- ○
- ○

PLAN

		○
		○
		○
		○
		○
		○
		○
		○
		○
		○
		○
		○
		○
		○
		○
		○
		○
		○
		○
		○
		○

TOTAL TIME	H	M
6		
7		
8		
9		
10		
11		
12		
1		
2		
3		
4		
5		
6		
7		
8		
9		
10		
11		
12		
1		
2		
3		
4		
5		

COMMENT

STUDY PLANNER

 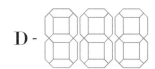
MOOD ☺ ☺ ☹ ☹ ☹	DATE.		MON	TUE	WED	THU	FRI	SAT	SUN

TODAY'S PRIORITY

- ○
- ○
- ○

PLAN	
	○
	○
	○
	○
	○
	○
	○
	○
	○
	○
	○
	○
	○
	○
	○
	○
	○
	○
	○
	○
	○

TOTAL TIME	H	M
6		
7		
8		
9		
10		
11		
12		
1		
2		
3		
4		
5		
6		
7		
8		
9		
10		
11		
12		
1		
2		
3		
4		
5		

COMMENT

STUDY PLANNER

 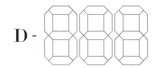

MOOD ☺ ☺ 😐 ☹ 😣	DATE.	MON	TUE	WED	THU	FRI	SAT	SUN

TODAY'S PRIORITY

○

○

○

PLAN			TOTAL TIME	H	M
		○			
		○	6		
		○	7		
		○	8		
		○	9		
		○	10		
		○	11		
		○	12		
		○	1		
		○	2		
		○	3		
		○	4		
		○	5		
		○	6		
		○	7		
		○	8		
		○	9		
		○	10		
		○	11		
			12		
			1		
			2		
			3		
			4		
			5		

COMMENT

STUDY PLANNER

D -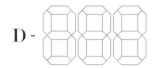

MOOD ☺ ☻ ☺ ☹ 😣	DATE.	MON	TUE	WED	THU	FRI	SAT	SUN

TODAY'S PRIORITY

○

○

○

PLAN			TOTAL TIME	H	M
		○			
		○	6		
		○	7		
		○	8		
		○	9		
		○	10		
		○	11		
		○	12		
		○	1		
		○	2		
		○	3		
		○	4		
		○	5		
		○	6		
		○	7		
		○	8		
		○	9		
		○	10		
		○	11		
			12		
			1		
			2		
			3		
			4		
			5		

COMMENT

STUDY PLANNER

D -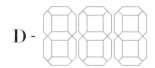

MOOD ☺ ☺ ☺ ☹ ☹	DATE.		MON	TUE	WED	THU	FRI	SAT	SUN

TODAY'S PRIORITY

○

○

○

PLAN			TOTAL TIME	H	M
	○	6			
	○	7			
	○	8			
	○	9			
	○	10			
	○	11			
	○	12			
	○	1			
	○	2			
	○	3			
	○	4			
	○	5			
	○	6			
	○	7			
	○	8			
	○	9			
	○	10			
	○	11			
		12			
		1			
		2			
		3			
		4			
		5			

COMMENT

STUDY PLANNER

D -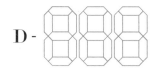

MOOD ☺ 😊 😐 🙁 😣	DATE.		MON	TUE	WED	THU	FRI	SAT	SUN

TODAY'S PRIORITY

○

○

○

PLAN		○
		○
		○
		○
		○
		○
		○
		○
		○
		○
		○
		○
		○
		○
		○
		○
		○
		○
		○
		○

TOTAL TIME	H	M
6		
7		
8		
9		
10		
11		
12		
1		
2		
3		
4		
5		
6		
7		
8		
9		
10		
11		
12		
1		
2		
3		
4		
5		

COMMENT

STUDY PLANNER

 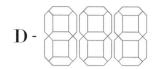

MOOD ☺☺☺☹☹	DATE.	MON	TUE	WED	THU	FRI	SAT	SUN

TODAY'S PRIORITY

- ○
- ○
- ○

PLAN		○
		○
		○
		○
		○
		○
		○
		○
		○
		○
		○
		○
		○
		○
		○
		○
		○
		○
		○

TOTAL TIME	H	M
6		
7		
8		
9		
10		
11		
12		
1		
2		
3		
4		
5		
6		
7		
8		
9		
10		
11		
12		
1		
2		
3		
4		
5		

COMMENT

STUDY PLANNER

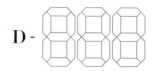

D -

MOOD ☺ 😄 😐 🙁 😣	DATE.		MON	TUE	WED	THU	FRI	SAT	SUN

TODAY'S PRIORITY

○

○

○

PLAN		○
		○
		○
		○
		○
		○
		○
		○
		○
		○
		○
		○
		○
		○
		○
		○
		○
		○
		○
		○

TOTAL TIME	H	M
6		
7		
8		
9		
10		
11		
12		
1		
2		
3		
4		
5		
6		
7		
8		
9		
10		
11		
12		
1		
2		
3		
4		
5		

COMMENT

STUDY PLANNER

 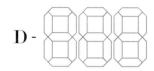

MOOD 😊 😀 😐 🙁 😣	DATE.	MON	TUE	WED	THU	FRI	SAT	SUN

TODAY'S PRIORITY

- ○
- ○
- ○

PLAN			TOTAL TIME	H	M
		○			
		○	6		
		○	7		
		○	8		
		○	9		
		○	10		
		○	11		
		○	12		
		○	1		
		○	2		
		○	3		
		○	4		
		○	5		
		○	6		
		○	7		
		○	8		
		○	9		
		○	10		
		○	11		
			12		
			1		
			2		
			3		
			4		
			5		

COMMENT

STUDY PLANNER

 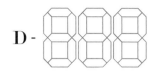

MOOD ☺ ☺ ☺ ☹ ☹	DATE.	MON	TUE	WED	THU	FRI	SAT	SUN

TODAY'S PRIORITY

○

○

○

PLAN		○
		○
		○
		○
		○
		○
		○
		○
		○
		○
		○
		○
		○
		○
		○
		○
		○
		○
		○
		○
		○

TOTAL TIME	H	M
6		
7		
8		
9		
10		
11		
12		
1		
2		
3		
4		
5		
6		
7		
8		
9		
10		
11		
12		
1		
2		
3		
4		
5		

COMMENT

STUDY PLANNER

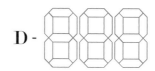

D -

MOOD ☺☺☺☹☹	DATE.		MON	TUE	WED	THU	FRI	SAT	SUN

TODAY'S PRIORITY

○

○

○

PLAN		
		○
		○
		○
		○
		○
		○
		○
		○
		○
		○
		○
		○
		○
		○
		○
		○
		○
		○
		○

TOTAL TIME	H	M
6		
7		
8		
9		
10		
11		
12		
1		
2		
3		
4		
5		
6		
7		
8		
9		
10		
11		
12		
1		
2		
3		
4		
5		

COMMENT

STUDY PLANNER

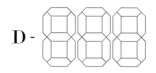

MOOD ☺☺☺☹☹	DATE.		MON	TUE	WED	THU	FRI	SAT	SUN

TODAY'S PRIORITY

○

○

○

PLAN		
		○
		○
		○
		○
		○
		○
		○
		○
		○
		○
		○
		○
		○
		○
		○
		○
		○
		○
		○
		○

TOTAL TIME	H	M
6		
7		
8		
9		
10		
11		
12		
1		
2		
3		
4		
5		
6		
7		
8		
9		
10		
11		
12		
1		
2		
3		
4		
5		

COMMENT

STUDY PLANNER

 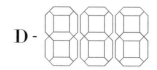

MOOD ☺ ☺ ☺ ☹ ☹	DATE.		MON	TUE	WED	THU	FRI	SAT	SUN

TODAY'S PRIORITY

○　.

○

○

PLAN		
		○
		○
		○
		○
		○
		○
		○
		○
		○
		○
		○
		○
		○
		○
		○
		○
		○
		○
		○
		○

TOTAL TIME	H	M
6		
7		
8		
9		
10		
11		
12		
1		
2		
3		
4		
5		
6		
7		
8		
9		
10		
11		
12		
1		
2		
3		
4		
5		

COMMENT